EXCEPTIONAL LEADER

How To Become Effective In Leading People And Managing Resources

ATTENTION: Thank you for your purchase!

If you are unhappy with your career or with people you are working with or leading, then I'd like to help you create a career breakthrough. I invite you to take advantage of a special, "Free Career Breakthrough" coaching session where we'll work together to...

1. Create a crystal-clear vision for your "ultimate career success" and the "perfect lifestyle" you'd like your career to provide.

2. Uncover hidden challenges that may be sabotaging your career growth and keeping you working too many hours with stress, overwhelm and burnout.

3. You will leave the session renewed, re-energized, and inspired to turn your career around for good with a flourishing personal life.

Call 02035070245, WhatsApp 07432319764 or email ray@connectoptions.co.uk

Connect with me on social media and ask me any question......

www.facebook.com/raykene
www.instagram.com/raykene1
www.linkedin.com/in/raykene

RAY KENE

Leadership & Success Mentor

EXCEPTIONAL LEADER

First Published in Great Britain in 2023
Ray Kene & Connect Options
27 Old Gloucester Street
London
WC1N 3AX
www.connectoptions.co.uk
www.inspire4success.com

This book is designed to provide information that the author believes to be accurate on the subject matter it covers, it is sold with the understanding that neither the author nor the publisher is offering individualized advice tailored to any specific portfolio or to any individual's particular needs or rendering investment advice or other professional services such as medical, legal or financial advice.

You should seek advice from a qualified doctor, lawyer or financial adviser. This book does not make any promise of earning potential which depends on factors outside of the control of the author and publishers.

No warranty is made with respect to the accuracy or completeness of the information contained herein, and both the author and the publisher specifically disclaim any responsibility for any liability, loss, or risk, personal or otherwise incurred as a consequence, directly or indirectly, of the use and application of any of the contents of this book.

British Library Cataloguing in Publication Data
ISBN: 9798872641582

CONTENTS AT A GLANCE

EMBRACING THE JOURNEY

In the pursuit of leadership, we often find ourselves navigating a path scattered with peaks of triumph and valleys of challenge. It is within these undulating terrains that our true leadership prowess is forged. This book, "Exceptional Leader," is not just about triumphing over obstacles; it's a testament to the transformative power of adversity in shaping exceptional leadership.

Throughout my career, I've encountered moments of exhilarating success and faced the daunting depths of failure. Each experience, whether a victory or a setback, has been an invaluable lesson in leadership. It's in these diverse landscapes of achievement and adversity that I discovered profound insights and honed the qualities that define exceptional leadership.

This book is not a roadmap to a flawless leadership journey. Instead, it's an honest and introspective exploration of how adversity, setbacks, and challenges can be catalysts for personal and leadership growth. It's a narrative that acknowledges the struggles, embraces the lessons learned, and celebrates the resilience required to emerge as a stronger, and more effective as a leader.

Inside this book, you'll find approaches of perseverance, strategies to navigate uncertainty, and styes on pivotal moments that can transform setbacks into stepping stones toward greater leadership efficacy.

I invite you on a journey of self-discovery, where the highs and lows of leadership can become integral parts of a transformative narrative.

As we embark on this exploration together, remember that leadership isn't solely about the destination—it's about the evolution, the resilience, and the wisdom gained along the way.

Whether you're a seasoned executive, an aspiring leader, or someone seeking inspiration in the face of adversity, this book aims to offer insights, strategies, and a roadmap toward becoming a better leader amidst life's myriad ups and downs.

Let's delve into the heart of leadership, learning from the styles, challenges, and emerging stronger, wiser, and more resilient on the other side.

Navigating The Path To Mastery

Welcome to the immersive journey of honing not just managerial skills but the art of leadership— where managing tasks converges with inspiring minds and hearts. "Exceptional Leader" is more than a mere guide; it's a testament to the transformative power of melding managerial prowess with visionary leadership.

In today's fast-paced and ever-evolving professional landscape, the roles of manager and leader intertwine in an intricate dance of strategy, empathy, vision, and adaptability. As someone deeply immersed in the realm of leadership and management, I've traversed the terrains of success and stumbled through the valleys of challenge.

This book is a culmination of insights gleaned from victories, setbacks, and the relentless pursuit of excellence. It's a blueprint born from the belief that leadership isn't merely a title; it's a commitment to continuous growth, learning, and the relentless pursuit of betterment.

But this isn't a monologue—it's a conversation, an exploration we embark upon together. Each chapter is an invitation to self-reflect, to glean insights from real-world experiences, and to embrace the art of becoming a better manager and a visionary leader.

Within the pages of this book lies a treasure trove of strategies, wisdom, and practical approaches to not just manage teams but to lead them toward greatness. We'll journey through the intricacies of effective communication, the nuances of team dynamics, and the fine art of balancing strategic vision with operational excellence.

If you're a seasoned executive seeking fresh perspectives or an emerging leader stepping into uncharted territory, this book is crafted to elevate your managerial acumen and infuse your leadership with inspiration.

This odyssey of management mastery intertwined with visionary leadership. Let's traverse the path that transcends the ordinary and forges a legacy of impactful leadership, leaving footprints of inspiration for generations to come.

The Fusion of Leadership And Management

There are two parts in this book, part one is about leadership while part two is about management.

In this book, we delve into the intersection where effective management converges with visionary leadership. "Exceptional Leader" is a voyage into the realms of management mastery and leadership excellence—an exploration of the delicate balance between steering the ship and charting the course.

In today's ever-evolving professional landscape, the roles of manager and leader intertwine to form the backbone of organizational success. Having navigated the diverse terrains of leadership challenges and managerial triumphs throughout my career, I've come to appreciate the symbiotic relationship between these two domains.

This book is a testament to the belief that exceptional leadership isn't just about steering a team—it's about cultivating a vision, inspiring greatness, and fostering an environment where individuals flourish, teams excel, and organizations thrive.

In this book, we embark on a journey that transcends conventional management manuals. We delve into the intricate nuances of effective delegation, strategic decision-making, nurturing talent, and inspiring change.

Yet, woven into these managerial facets is the thread of visionary leadership—inspiring, motivating, and guiding teams toward a shared vision of success.

This isn't a book just about theories and principles; it's a practical guide enriched with real-world approaches, actionable strategies, and reflective styles designed to empower you on your path toward managerial and leadership excellence.

Whether you're a seasoned manager aiming to refine your leadership edge or an aspiring leader ready to embark on a transformative journey, this book aims to be your compass—a companion that equips you with the tools, insights, and mindset needed to evolve into a better manager and a visionary leader.

Join me as we navigate the waters of management mastery and leadership brilliance. Let's embrace the fusion of management and leadership and embark on a transformative journey that doesn't just redefine how you manage, but how you lead and inspire those around you.

PART ONE: LEADERSHIP

Becoming A Better Leader

CHAPTER 1: CONCEPT OF LEADERSHIP

INTRODUCTION

Napoleon Hill once said: "One bad general does better than two good ones." It takes a moment for the sense of this to register, but it is the same as our modern saying that "too many cooks spoil the broth".

Having one set of instructions, even if they are flawed, is preferable to having two sets of perfect directions that, when enacted together without reference to each other, cause havoc. This is the principle of leadership in a nutshell. It is all about maintaining focus and creating positive outcomes.

The same can be applied to individuals who strive to become leaders. There needs to be focus and determination. Advice can be given but does not have to be heeded.

History is full of leaders whose beginnings were disastrous, and had they listened to the naysayers of this world, they would not have succeeded in becoming better leaders and our world wouldn't have made any much progress, though a lot still need to be done, the world has evolved overtime.

Leadership can be learned. Some people are certainly born with leadership skills, but this is not a prerequisite for becoming a leader. Instead, dedication to the art of leadership is more important. Leadership involves understanding how to inspire, influence and control how people behave.

It is not a simple matter of shouting or having a deep and booming voice; or being great in physical stature. Gandhi possessed none of these attributes but managed to lead a nation and inspire millions around the world.

Sometimes, leadership may be no more than having a poignant message for a receptive audience at an opportune moment. Of itself, leadership is neither good nor bad; the world has known more than its fair share of evil and charismatic dictators.

In the world of business, the perception of leadership has changed from its early days when it largely mirrored the military model of leadership from the top down, with powerful individuals dominating large groups of less powerful people.

Nowadays, leadership in business is far more knowledge driven. The lowliest employee may end up effectively leading the direction of a vast corporation through his or her innovative ideas. Anyone with critical knowledge can show leadership.

This is known as thought-leadership. In other situations, leadership can be about taking a stand for what you believe in and trying to convince people to think and act differently.

Leadership has been variously described as the "process of social influence in which one person can enlist the aid and support of others in the accomplishment of a common task".

"Creating a way for people to contribute to making something extraordinary happen"; "the ability to successfully integrate and maximize available resources within the internal and external environment for the attainment of organizational or societal goals".

And "the capacity of leaders to listen and observe, to use their expertise as a starting point to encourage dialogue between all levels of decision-making, to establish processes and transparency in decision-making, to articulate their own values and visions clearly but not impose them".

Leadership is about setting and not just reacting to agendas, identifying problems, and initiating change that makes for substantive improvement rather than managing change.

Leadership is a multifaceted concept that involves guiding and influencing others to achieve common goals, create change, or navigate towards a shared vision. At its core, leadership is about:

1. Inspiring And Influencing

Leaders motivate and inspire individuals or groups, encouraging them to move in a particular direction or work towards a shared objective.

2. Setting Vision And Direction

Effective leaders articulate a clear vision, defining the purpose and direction for their team or organization. They communicate this vision in a way that resonates with others and provides a roadmap for action.

3. Empowering Others

Leaders empower their team members by fostering an environment of trust, collaboration, and autonomy. They delegate responsibilities, encourage growth, and provide support to enable others to reach their full potential.

4. Making Decisions And Taking Initiative

Leaders often make critical decisions, take calculated risks, and initiate necessary changes.

They demonstrate decisiveness and adaptability in navigating challenges and uncertainties.

5. Influencing Change And Innovation

Leaders drive innovation, encourage creative thinking, and facilitate adaptation to changes in the environment or industry.

6. Being An Example

Leadership involves modelling the behaviours, values, and ethics expected from others. Leaders set an example through their actions, integrity, and commitment to the shared vision.

Leadership can manifest in various contexts, including business, politics, education, community organizations, and more. It's not limited to formal titles or positions but can emerge from anyone who demonstrates the ability to inspire, guide, and influence others towards a common goal or purpose.

Effective leadership often involves a blend of interpersonal skills, emotional intelligence, strategic thinking, and a deep understanding of the needs and motivations of the people being led.

TYPES OF LEADERSHIP

Leadership has a variety of different concept, and various types of leadership have emerged over time, each emphasizing different approaches to guiding and influencing individuals or groups.

Types of leadership typically refer to broader categories or overarching paradigms of leadership, emphasizing different approaches or overarching philosophies.

In essence, types of leadership are broader concepts or paradigms that encapsulate fundamental principles or philosophies guiding leadership. Leaders often draw from various types of leadership based on their guiding principles.

FOUR TYPES OF LEADERSHIP

Authentic Leadership

Authentic leaders lead by being true to themselves, displaying transparency, and aligning their actions with their values. They build trust through openness, self-awareness, and consistency between their words and actions.

Servant Leadership

Servant leaders prioritize serving others first, focusing on the needs of their team members before their own. They emphasize empathy, listening, and supporting the growth and development of their followers.

Transactional Leadership

Transactional leaders focus on maintaining the status quo and achieving specific goals through a system of rewards and punishments. They emphasize clear structures, routines, and exchange-based relationships where followers are rewarded for meeting goals and expectations.

Transformational Leadership

Transformational leaders inspire and motivate their teams or followers by creating a compelling vision, encouraging innovation, and fostering a sense of commitment to organizational goals. They often focus on individual development, empowerment, and long-term change.

They lead by example, often exhibiting charisma, enthusiasm, and a strong commitment to their vision. These leaders empower their teams by encouraging creativity, fostering a positive work environment, and setting high standards.

They often develop strong emotional connections with their followers and are skilled at influencing and motivating them to achieve extraordinary results.

So, transformational, transactional, servant, and authentic leadership are considered types of leadership. These types often encompass a set of principles, values, and guiding philosophies that define the nature and direction of leadership.

These leadership types represent a spectrum of approaches, each with its strengths and limitations. Effective leaders often employ a blend of these styles, adapting their approach based on the situation, context, and the needs of their team to achieve optimal results.

STYLES OF LEADERSHIP

Leadership styles represent the varying approaches that leaders use to guide and influence individuals or groups. Styles of leadership refer to specific ways or methods that leaders employ to interact with and influence their teams or followers.

These styles represent the behavioural patterns or approaches that leaders adopt in their day-to-day interactions and decision-making processes.

Styles of leadership represent specific behaviours or approaches that leaders adopt within those broader paradigms to interact with their teams or followers. Leaders may adapt their styles of leadership based on situational needs, team dynamics, or the specific context they are facing.

SIX COMMON STYLES OF LEADERSHIP

Democratic Leadership

Democratic leaders involve their team members in decision-making, encouraging participation, collaboration, and shared responsibility. This approach fosters a sense of ownership, empowerment, and engagement among team members.

They value input from their team and seek consensus and often leverage the collective knowledge and expertise of the team before making decisions.

Laissez-faire leadership

Laissez-faire leaders provide considerable freedom to their team members, offering minimal guidance or interference in decision-making. This style allows for autonomy and self-direction but might require highly skilled and motivated individuals.

While this style can empower skilled and self-motivated individuals, it may lead to confusion or lack of direction in situations where team members require guidance or support.

Autocratic Leadership

Autocratic leaders make decisions independently without consulting their team members. They provide clear instructions and expect strict adherence to their directives.

This style can be efficient in certain situations that require quick decision-making, clear guidance, or in certain hierarchical structures. However, it may hinder creativity, autonomy, and motivation among team members due to the lack of participation in decision-making.

Bureaucratic Leadership

Bureaucratic leaders adhere strictly to established rules, procedures, and hierarchies. They focus on maintaining order, efficiency, and stability within the organization.

Charismatic Leadership

Charismatic leaders possess a strong personality and charm that inspires and motivates followers. They often exhibit confidence, enthusiasm, and a compelling vision, drawing others toward their cause through their magnetism.

Situational Leadership

Situational leaders adapt their leadership style based on the readiness and development level of their followers or the specific situation at hand. They adjust their approach to match the needs and capabilities of their team.

The above styles focus on how leaders communicate, make decisions, and engage with their teams. Each style has its strengths and limitations and can be effective in different contexts.

Effective leaders often blend these styles, choosing the most suitable approach depending on the situation, the needs of their team, and the objectives they aim to achieve.

CHAPTER 2: MODELS AND APPROACHES

SITUATIONAL LEADERSHIP MODEL

Situational Leadership is a leadership model developed by Paul Hersey and Ken Blanchard in the late 1960s and early 1970s. This model focuses on the idea that effective leadership is flexible and should adapt to the needs of the followers or team members based on the specific situation or context.

The Situational Leadership Theory (SLT) suggests that there is no one-size-fits-all approach to leadership. Instead, it emphasizes that leaders should adjust their leadership style based on the competence and commitment levels of their team and followers in a given task or situation.

The model identifies four primary leadership styles and suggests that leaders should choose the most appropriate style based on the readiness level of their followers:

Directing/Telling (S1)

In this style, the leader provides clear instructions, closely supervises tasks, and makes decisions without consulting followers. This style is suitable for individuals or teams who are new to a task or lack the necessary skills or confidence to perform it.
'

Coaching/Selling (S2)

This style involves more two-way communication, with the leader providing guidance and explanations to help followers understand their roles and tasks better.

Leaders adopting this style aim to persuade and support followers who are learning and gaining confidence in their abilities.

Supporting/Participating (S3)

Here, the leader delegates more responsibility to the followers, allowing them to take a more active role in decision-making. The leader supports and facilitates their progress while encouraging collaboration and shared decision-making.

Delegating/Sending (S4)

In this style, the leader gives followers autonomy and allows them to make decisions independently. The leader provides minimal supervision and trusts the followers' competence and commitment to handle tasks effectively.

The Situational Leadership model proposes that the readiness level of followers can be assessed based on their competence (skills and knowledge) and commitment (motivation and confidence) for a specific task.

Leaders should then adjust their leadership style accordingly to match the readiness level of their team members.

The essence of Situational Leadership lies in the leader's ability to diagnose the situation and adapt their style to best suit the needs of their followers, promoting development, maximizing performance, and fostering a supportive and adaptive work environment.

Mastering Situational Leadership: Adapting Styles for Optimal Results

Leadership isn't a one-size-fits-all concept; it's a dynamic interplay between adapting to situations and leveraging diverse leadership styles to maximize team performance.

Situational leadership, popularized by management experts Ken Blanchard and Paul Hersey, revolves around the idea that effective leadership isn't about adhering to a singular style, but rather adapting leadership approaches based on the situation and the needs of the team.

This model identifies four primary leadership styles—coaching, supporting, directing, and delegating—each suited for different situations and stages of team development. Let's explore these styles and their applications in nurturing high-performing teams:

1. Coaching: Empowering Through Guidance

Coaching as a leadership style involves providing guidance, support, and development opportunities to team members. It's most effective when individuals have the willingness to learn and grow.

A coaching leader invests time in understanding their team members' strengths, weaknesses, and aspirations. They provide feedback, mentorship, and resources to help team members improve their skills and achieve their goals.

This style encourages personal growth, fosters self-confidence, and empowers individuals to take ownership of their development.

2. Supporting: Fostering Confidence And Collaboration

Supportive leadership focuses on nurturing relationships, building trust, and fostering a positive work environment.

Leaders adopting a supportive style focus on empathetic listening, providing encouragement, and helping when needed. This style is particularly beneficial during periods of change, uncertainty, or when team morale needs a boost.

Supporting leaders prioritize collaboration, create a sense of belonging, and ensure team members feel valued, leading to increased engagement and motivation.

3. Directing: Providing Clarity And Structure

Directing leadership style involves giving clear instructions, setting expectations, and closely supervising tasks. It's most effective when team members lack experience or when urgent decisions need to be made.
Directing leaders provide specific guidance, outline objectives, and closely monitor progress. This style helps in aligning team efforts toward achieving immediate goals and ensures clarity in roles and responsibilities, especially in new or challenging situations.

4. Delegating: Empowering Autonomy And Accountability

Delegating as a leadership style empowers team members by giving them autonomy and decision-making authority.

Leaders who delegate effectively trust their team's capabilities, assign tasks based on individual strengths, and provide necessary support while allowing freedom to execute responsibilities.

This style encourages innovation, fosters a sense of ownership, and allows leaders to focus on higher-level strategic initiatives.

Understanding these four leadership styles allows managers to assess the readiness and development level of their team members, enabling them to adapt their approach accordingly.

Effective situational leadership involves a blend of these styles, applied contextually based on the specific needs of the team and the objectives at hand.

As leaders navigate the complexities of their roles, mastering the art of situational leadership becomes a cornerstone of driving team success and fostering a culture of continuous growth, achievement and transformation.

TRANSFORMATIONAL LEADERSHIP

Transformational leadership is a leadership approach that focuses on inspiring and motivating followers to achieve exceptional outcomes.

It is coined by James MacGregor Burns in the 1970s and expanded upon by Bernard Bass, this approach revolves around the leader's ability to bring about significant change, transformation, and growth within individuals and organizations.

Six Key Characteristics Of Transformational Leadership

Vision And Inspiration

Transformational leaders articulate a compelling vision of the future that inspires and motivates followers. They create a shared sense of purpose, instilling enthusiasm and commitment toward common goals.

Charisma And Influence

These leaders often exhibit charismatic qualities, exuding confidence, enthusiasm, and a magnetic personality that draws others to them. They use their influence to inspire trust and rally people around a shared vision.

Individualized Consideration

Transformational leaders pay attention to the individual needs, strengths, and aspirations of their followers. They offer support, coaching, and mentorship, fostering a personalized approach to development.

Intellectual Stimulation

These leaders encourage creativity, innovation, and critical thinking among their team members. Transformational leaders challenge the status quo, stimulate new ideas, and create an environment that values intellectual growth.

Empowerment And Delegation

These leaders empower their followers, granting them autonomy, and delegating authority. They encourage individuals to take ownership of their work and decision-making processes.

Emotional Intelligence

Transformational leaders possess high emotional intelligence, understanding and empathizing with the emotions of their team members. They use emotions positively to motivate and inspire rather than manipulate.

Transformational leaders often stand out in their ability to create a positive and empowering work culture. They foster a climate of trust, encourage open communication, and cultivate an environment where team members feel valued, motivated, and empowered to achieve not only individual success but also the collective goals of the organization.

The impact of transformational leadership goes beyond immediate results; it nurtures long-term growth, enhances organizational resilience, and fosters a culture of continuous improvement. This leadership style has been associated with higher levels of employee engagement, job satisfaction, and organizational commitment.

While transformational leadership can inspire positive change, it's crucial to note that it might not be the most effective approach in all situations. Different contexts and challenges may require a blend of leadership styles to achieve optimal outcomes.

Nonetheless, transformational leadership remains a powerful force for driving organizational success by igniting passion, innovation, and commitment among followers.

TRANSFORMATIVE LEADERSHIP

Transformative leadership shares similarities with transformational leadership but expands its focus beyond individual and organizational change. This approach of leadership encompasses a broader scope, emphasizing social change, justice, and equity, aiming to address systemic issues and create a positive impact on a larger scale.

Key Characteristics Of Transformative Leadership Include:

Social Change Orientation

Transformative leaders are committed to addressing societal challenges, advocating for social justice, and driving meaningful change at a community, societal, or even global level. They prioritize initiatives that aim to improve society's well-being and address systemic inequalities.

Empowerment And Inclusivity

These leaders empower marginalized voices, advocate for inclusivity, and promote diversity. They create environments that respect and value different perspectives, fostering a culture of inclusiveness and equity.

Collaborative And Participative Approach

Transformative leaders encourage collaboration among diverse stakeholders. They seek input and involvement from various groups affected by social issues, promoting collective action and shared responsibility for change.

Critical Reflection And Awareness

They encourage critical thinking, self-reflection, and awareness of societal issues among their followers. These leaders foster a culture of inquiry, encouraging individuals to question the status quo and challenge social norms.

Ethical And Moral Grounding

Transformative leadership is grounded in strong ethical and moral principles. Leaders in this realm prioritize ethical behaviour, transparency, and accountability, guiding their actions with a sense of social responsibility.

Long-Term Vision And Sustainable Change

These leaders have a vision for sustainable change, focusing on long-term solutions rather than short-term fixes. They aim to create lasting and meaningful impact, addressing root causes rather than just symptoms of societal issues.

Transformative leadership extends beyond organizational boundaries, aiming to create a more just and equitable society. While it can encompass aspects of transformational leadership—inspiring change and fostering growth—its primary focus lies in effecting societal transformations and tackling systemic challenges that impact communities and larger societal structures.

This style of leadership is often seen in social activists, community organizers, and leaders in nonprofit organizations or movements dedicated to social justice, equity, environmental sustainability, and human rights. Transformative leaders strive to create a world where fairness, equality, and social well-being are at the forefront of collective consciousness and action.

Difference Between Transformational Leadership And Transformative Leadership

The difference between transformational and transformative leadership lies primarily in their focus, emphasis and impact:

Focus

Transformational leadership focuses on inspiring and motivating individuals or organizations to achieve exceptional results or growth.

It involves inspiring followers, articulating a compelling vision, and motivating them to exceed expectations.

Transformative leadership has a broader focus, extending beyond individual or organizational change to encompass societal or systemic transformations. It aims to address larger social issues, advocate for social justice, and create positive change on a wider scale.

Emphasis

Transformational style concentrates on personal and organizational change. Transformational leaders aim to transform individuals and teams by fostering a shared vision, encouraging innovation, and promoting personal growth.

Transformative style emphasizes on social change, inclusivity, and equity. Transformative leaders work to empower marginalized voices, advocate for systemic change, and foster collaboration among diverse stakeholders to address societal issues.

Impact

The impact of transformational leadership tends to be within the context of organizations or groups, fostering motivation, higher performance, and a positive organizational culture.

Transformative leadership seeks to impact communities, societies, or even global systems. Its focus extends to promoting social justice, equity, and addressing systemic inequalities beyond organizational boundaries.

Summary

In essence, while both leadership styles aim to bring about change, transformational leadership focuses on personal and organizational growth, often within an organizational context.

On the other hand, transformative leadership emphasizes broader social change, seeking to address systemic issues, societal inequalities, and social justice concerns on a larger scale, often extending beyond organizational or group boundaries.

Leadership Practice of Authenticity, Service, Ethics, And Spirituality

Leadership isn't merely about holding a title; it's a dynamic and transformative force that shapes organizational culture, inspires individuals, and drives change. In the realm of leadership theory and practice, several paradigms stand out for their emphasis on authenticity, service, ethics, and spirituality as guiding principles.

Authentic Leadership: Leading From The Core

Authentic leadership revolves around leaders being true to themselves, displaying transparency, and aligning their actions with their values and beliefs.

These leaders prioritize self-awareness, genuine interactions, and building trusting relationships with their teams. They inspire through their authenticity, fostering an environment where individuals feel valued and empowered.

Servant Leadership: Serving To Empower

Servant leadership centres on the idea that leaders serve their teams first. They prioritize the needs of their followers, empower them, and facilitate their growth and success.

These leaders exhibit empathy, actively listen to their team members, and aim to make a positive impact on their lives and the broader community.

Ethical Leadership: Upholding Integrity And Values

Ethical leadership places a strong emphasis on integrity, moral principles, and ethical decision-making. Leaders in this paradigm set high ethical standards, model ethical behaviour, and create a culture of transparency and accountability.

They navigate complex ethical dilemmas with fairness and uphold values that guide the organization's actions.

Spiritual Leadership: Inspiring Through Purpose And Meaning

Spiritual leadership transcends traditional boundaries, focusing on the higher purpose and meaning within organizational contexts. Leaders in this realm inspire by connecting individuals to a shared vision or purpose that goes beyond financial success.

They foster a sense of belonging, encourage personal growth, and infuse the workplace with a deeper sense of meaning.

Summary

Embracing these transformative leadership paradigms doesn't mean adhering strictly to one style but rather integrating the principles into a holistic leadership approach.

Leaders can draw upon the authenticity of their actions, the service-oriented mindset, ethical decision-making, and the search for deeper meaning to create a more profound impact.

Leadership that encompasses authenticity, service, ethics, and spirituality offers a pathway to creating vibrant, engaged teams and nurturing organizational cultures where individuals thrive. By embracing these principles, leaders become catalysts for positive change, driving not just performance but also fostering environments of trust, purpose, and ethical conduct.

In the tapestry of leadership, the threads of authenticity, service, ethics, and spirituality weave together to create a canvas of transformative leadership—one that inspires, empowers, and leaves an enduring legacy of positive influence.

CHAPTER 3: INFLUENCE AND MINDSET

HOW TO LEAD AND INFLUENCE PEOPLE

Leading people has nothing to do with managing them. Too many managers are trying to micro-manage their team but forgetting to lead them effectively.

If you want to become a strong leader, you need to lead by example. This means you must show your team that you are perfectly capable to set examples. By doing so, you will earn their respect and create lifelong devotees who would move mountains to please you.

Conversely, a manager who hides behind his office door while commanding staff isn't going to gain much respect in the workplace.

Ultimately the success of any business venture lies in the hands of its employees and NOT the managers. A manager's responsibility is to organize and manage business systems, systems that will see to the successful finalization of projects.

If your staff are unhappy, it will soon show in their lack of productivity. This will influence your bottom line. Chances are customer complaints will start to amass and office gossip will run hot. This is counterproductive to running a well-oiled machine, which is your business.

It's All About Relationships

No organization can function very well without the co-operation of its employees. Unfortunately, the necessity in any organization is that there are various levels of status within the team, and this can lead to conflicts if not managed properly.

An effective leader should realize that the team under them is there because they must be. Most employees work to earn money, not because they enjoy the daily grind of a nine-to-five/work.

For this reason, there must be an effort to build healthy relationships, or life in the workplace can become untenable for everyone, and productivity will decline.

Leaders need to make their workplace function positively, with cooperation and respect. In this way, everyone is working for the common good and towards a common purpose. This demands that effective relationships are built upon an understanding of each other's needs.

It is no different to how things should be in the home; no personal relationship will last very long if there is a sense that one or both parties are being selfish.

The most effective way to understand how other people are feeling is to listen to what they have to say. This must be done without judging, and not as though you are being forced to do so by some higher authority.

Very often, teams will have the same goals as their leaders, but may just want to know that they are not seen as automatons that have no creative input.

Quality workplace relationships make people feel happy. One of the major reasons why employees move on from a company is because of relationship clashes with leaders or other colleagues.

Leaders should also make sure that they create the circumstances for understanding within their team, and this means asking questions.

If your team will simply pipe up and express their feelings is not enough; many people will not feel it is their place to speak up unless they are specifically asked to do so.

Listening should be done attentively, not glancing at your watch every couple of minutes or trying not to look bored. This means you listen without interrupting or fidgeting, and with the correct expression.

Your expression should be genuine, or you will be found out very quickly and the situation will become worse than had you not asked in the first place.

A great way to foster healthy relationships with your team is by meeting them in a more social environment on regular occasions. Some companies choose to send their staff to regular golfing, outings, while others prefer to host a regular BBQ or weekend trips.

Regardless of what you end up choosing, the key lies in giving your team a chance to connect away from the daily grind. Building effective relationships means that neither party should make any assumptions.

As a leader, you cannot expect people to understand exactly what we want and why you want it. Sometimes it is this lack of comprehension that causes problems. As much as you must trust your team members to have intelligence, if they are not party to the goals you are working towards, they can become resistant.

As far as possible, your team should be conversant with your goals and how their actions are contributing to their successful outcome. Humans are inquisitive and function better when not kept in the dark.

Respect is the key ingredient of any good relationship, and this means respect for yourself as well as others. Genuinely listening and understanding are the ways in which you show that you respect the person you are talking to.

Quickly judging based on preconceived ideas or prejudice is the opposite of having respect. Bear in mind that not everyone will respond in 100% perfect fashion to all that occurs in the workplace.

Although it is not the leader's job to be a permanent shoulder to cry on, it is important to accept that your team is made up of individuals whose lives may not be as perfect as their coffee   break banter might lead you to believe.

Whilst creating a healthy working relationship is a crucial goal, the smart leader will always bear in mind that conflict is inevitable and must be managed, rather than ignored for the sake of apparent peace.

Relationships can never improve unless problems are identified and confronted. Differences between people are inevitable and hearing them aired can lead to some very useful resolutions that produce ideas beyond the expected.

The alternative is highly detrimental, which is to let problems fester and build, and ruin the atmosphere in a workplace, if not productivity levels. Do all that is needed to avoid such ugly situation.

Keys To Good Working Relationships

1. One party at least should value the relationship – This may start off as a one-way street, but this can lead to a meeting of minds later.

2. Listen effectively, without judging – Listening in this way will promote mutual understanding and mutual respect.

3. Have informal chats – Chatting over a coffee can encourage a franker exchange of views than meeting officially with a desk between you.

4. Create an open culture – Your team should know they can speak freely, no matter if that is to express happiness, joy, contentment, anger, irritation, sadness or fear. Negative feelings that are hoarded cause significant problems.

MINDSET: EMPOWERING OTHERS

Leaders must take responsibility for their team's performance, which means leaders must be happy that the direction of their team is one which they think is best.

Although it is useful to have creative sessions with team members to bat around a few ideas, the overarching goals that the team must fulfil are most often set by the leader, or some authority above the leader.

The challenge is therefore to get the team "onside" with the given aims, even when some team members may wholeheartedly disagree with them, or baulk at the idea that these have been imposed on them from above.

Despite the accepted hierarchy of any workplace, for a team to work most efficiently, its members – especially high-level ones may feel they are contributing more than the spade work. They may feel that they have chosen where some of the plots should be dug.

This presents a challenge for the leader who cannot just let his or her subordinates have free play. The team must be made to feel involved and motivated. Otherwise, the situation can become worse, and your team will show a little or much disobedience.

You must be thinking, how then do I provoke a positive response in them? The answer is by empowering your team, as far as possible. Short of handing over the reins and heading off home.

An inspirational and motivational leader must be able to create a sense that their team is actively involved in the process and contributing in a real sense to the overall outcome of the project.

This can involve learning how to make your suggestions appeal to them. This may mean you solicit their opinions and take the best ideas on board. Or you may have to convince them that your goals are shared and that their futures are tied to your overall success.

It may be a simple matter of making an employee understand that their job will be safer if they perform well; reminding them that they are working for themselves and their family, and not just for a company.

However, empowering others does not just mean employing tactics that persuade other people to your own opinion or goals. It can also mean demonstrating leadership qualities that inspire others to act at their very best, no matter what is asked of them.

Such leadership qualities would be most evidenced in the armed services, where the result of potentially being killed is rarely going to elicit a whoop and a cheer. Soldiers are empowered to greatness by the examples set by their commanding officers.

Sometimes, it is just a matter of being an admirable and inspirational human being. Of course, some are born with more of these qualities than others, but we can all strive to lead by example, so that others will feel empowered to make great things happen.

GETTING THE MOST FROM YOUR TEAM

Start Right

When a staff member joins your team, give them time to become fully acclimatized to your company. The sooner they settle, the sooner you can start to reap rewards.

It will help if you complete an induction and a detailed contract of employment, which outlines what you expect from them.

Create Expectations

Strange as it may sound, some employees do not have a clear sense of their role. Such confusion can cause arguments, or even duplication or omission of tasks. This is clearly bad for productivity. Your team needs to know their job and responsibilities; a job description will help.

Stand Back

Part of empowering your team is trusting they can get on with the job without you peering over their shoulder every fifteen minutes. If you want staff members to flourish, they should be allowed to get on with their job.

Of course, you need to keep a watchful eye, but there is a happy medium where they know you trust them. Your team is more likely to over-perform if they feel good about what they are doing. Motivated staff work harder.

Money is often not the prime motivator. They want to know what is expected of them, and then they want to be allowed to get on with it. This is far easier if the right people are employed in the first place.

Communication

Effective communication is the lifeblood of any organization, regardless of its size. That may mean face-to-face talks or pinning notes on a board.

Provided your team knows what's going on, you are being an effective leader. Try asking your team how they prefer communication to happen. This helps to empower them.

Keep Communicating

It can happen that there is a sincere intention to improve communication, and it all starts off positively: team briefs, newsletters; intranets, etc. Then things start to slow down.

As a leader you should not let this happen. It may mean important information is not imparted, or you are viewed as not bothered how the team is getting on.

Be Honest

Communication is not much use if your team believes it is not getting the whole picture. Bad news is still news, and you must trust that your people are mature enough to handle it, or you may find they are insulted and no longer believe what you tell them.

This does not mean shouting every piece of office gossip from the rooftop, but it does mean keeping your team abreast of all that is pertinent to them.

Consultation

Effective consultation is a vital tool to improving performance. Your team members have specific roles. Your collective overview may be more knowledgeable, but there may be team members whose specific knowledge is greater than yours.

Asking for their opinion is not weak; it is sensible, and it serves to empower that team member. The more facts you have, the easier and more effective your decision-making will be. Getting the most out of your team is greatly aided by effective consultation and it demonstrates respect from you to them.

Training

Training is a boon if it is relevant to the team members receiving it. You are guaranteed to alienate staff by sending them on courses that bear no relevance to their role. Training for the sake of training is counterproductive. You need to ask:

> ➢ Will the training help the business?

> ➢ Is it geared to the priorities of the business?

> ➢ Are the right individuals and teams within your organization receiving the training?

> ➢ How can I quantify any improvement?

Training must be organized and delivered effectively, or you should not commit to it in the first place. Ensure that the agreed priorities are met. Once this happens, think how you can help individual team members in their personal development. This can be a real aid towards improving performance and motivation.

When the training is over, try and evaluate its worth. Where do you expect to see improvements? If you evaluate effectively, you can judge where further investment in training will pay off.

Organizations of all sizes invest in their people through effective training. Your team is your most valuable asset, and their performance has an impact on the company's bottom line.

Staff Appraisals

All companies should review performance of their staff on a regular basis. When staff appraisals do not work, it is because of one or more of for the reasons below.

There is no system in place for undertaking reviews on a regular basis; there is no paper trail to follow so people don't know where to start; they are used purely to air grievances, so it becomes a negative thing; the appraiser isn't trained to appraise so the results are unreliable; there is no follow-up, so improvements are missed.

CHAPTER 4: DARK SIDE OF LEADERSHIP

What we have discussed so far apply to the ideals of leadership. But why has leadership gone awry?

The dark side of any individual when allowed to go unchecked can create a rigid and dysfunctional personality that stifles creativity, taints or ruins relationships. When such characteristics are given reign in a leader, a self-righteous and bombastic person can result, who alienates the very people they are meant to inspire.

The Compulsive Leader

Compulsive leaders feel like they must do everything themselves. They try to manage every aspect of their business, often refusing to delegate, and cannot resist having their say on everything. As they lack trust in others, they cannot let anyone else take responsibility, therefore they restrict personal growth in their team.

Compulsive leaders have many other traits. They are perfectionists who must follow highly rigid and systematized daily routines and are concerned with status. Thus, they strive to impress their superiors with their diligence and efficiency and continually look for reassurance and approval.

This can lead to them becoming workaholics, and their team is viewed as failing if they don't keep pace. Spontaneity is not encouraged as these bucks the routine.

Despite this appearance of total control, such leaders can be fit to explode on the inside, and this can be the result of a childhood environment where unrealistic expectations were placed on them.

Their attempts to keep control are linked to their attempts to suppress anger and resentment, which makes them susceptible to outbursts of temper if they perceive they are losing their grip.

The Narcissistic Leader

Narcissistic leaders are focused on themselves. Life and the world revolve around them, and they must be at the centre of all that is happening. Whilst they exaggerate their own merits, they will try to ignore the merits of others, or seek to devalue them, because other people's accomplishments are seen as a threat to their own standing.

The worst type of narcissistic leader cannot tolerate even a hint of criticism and disagreement and avoid their self-delusions and fantasies being undermined by surrounding themselves with sycophants.

Where possible, they will attempt to use the merits of others for their own advancement and think nothing of stepping on people to get ahead. Their own feeling of self-importance means they are unable to empathize with those in their team, because they cannot feel any connection.

Their only focus is on receiving plaudits that further bolster their sense of greatness. Such an attitude is often the result of a deep-seated inferiority complex, and thus no matter how much they are achieving, they will never feel it is enough.

Some narcissistic leaders take on a sidekick, but this person is expected to always toe the line and serves only to reflect glory onto them and loudly approve of all that they do. Clever sidekicks can subtly manipulate the leader into focusing on the operational outcome of their plans, rather than just their own self-aggrandizement.

Ultimately, this type of leader can be very successful if their vision is strong, and they get the organization to identify with them and think like they do. Such productive narcissists have more perspective and can step back and even laugh at their own irrational needs.

The Paranoid Leader

Paranoid leaders are exactly as they sound. Paranoid that other people are better than they are, and thus they view even the mildest criticism as devastating.

They are liable to overreact if they sense they are being attacked, especially in front of other people. This can manifest itself in open hostility. This attitude is the result of an inferiority complex that perceives even the most constructive criticism in the wrong way.

The paranoid leader will be guarded in their dealings with other people because they do not want to reveal too much of themselves in case, they display their weaknesses and are attacked or undermined.

They may be scared that their position is undeserved, therefore can be deeply suspicious of colleagues who may steal their limelight or perhaps challenge for their position. This is not always a wholly negative trait.

However. a healthy dose of paranoia can be key to success in business, because it helps keep leaders on their toes, always aware of opportunities not to be missed. It is the opposite end of the spectrum to being complacent and can make for a very successful venture.

The Codependent Leader

Co-dependent leaders do not enjoy taking the lead, and instead seek to copy what others have done or are doing. They avoid confrontation and would rather cover up problems than face them head-on.

Planning is not their forte. They tend instead to react to whatever comes their way, rather than acting to alter outcomes or achieve goals. Codependent leaders, therefore, are not leaders at all.

They are reactionary and have the habit of keeping important information to themselves because they are not prepared to act upon it. This can clearly lead to poor outcomes because all the pertinent facts are not known to those below the leader who may be charged with making decisions.

This type of leader avoids confrontation and is thus liable to accept a greater workload for themselves rather than respond negatively to any request. They are also prone to accepting the blame for situations they have not caused.

The Passive-Aggressive Leader

Passive-aggressive leaders feel like they need to control everything, and when they can't they cause problems for those who are in control. However, they are sneaky in their ploys, and are very difficult to catch out.

Their main characteristics are that they can be stubborn, purposely forgetful, intentionally inefficient, complaining (behind closed doors), and they parry demands put on them through procrastination.

Typically, if they feel they are not firmly in the driving seat, they will jump out and puncture the tires when no one is looking, then feign horror and pretend to search around for a tire iron.

This type of leader has two speeds: full speed ahead and stopped. When situations do not go their way, they will offer their full support for whatever has been decided, then gossip and back stab, wilfully cause delays, and generally create upset.

When confronted, they claim to have been misinterpreted. Passive aggressive leader is often chronically late for appointments, using any excuse to dominate and regain some control of the situation.

Dealing with passive-aggressive leaders is thus a draining and frustrating affair that saps energy. They are not averse to short outbursts of sadness or anger to regain some control but are ultimately fearful of success since it leads to higher expectations.

CHAPTER 5: EXCEPTIONAL LEADER

HOW TO BECOME EXCEPTIONAL LEADER

1. Ask To Be Judged

Finding out what others think of your leadership skills can really help you change for the better. Sometimes leaders can be so wrapped up in appraising others, that they do not seek appraisal from below, only from their own superiors.

Your team is the best source of feedback, because they are on the receiving end of your "skills" every day. Honesty should be encouraged, but bear in mind that it may only be anonymous feedback that holds the truth if your team believes you are going to use it against them or become defensive about what they say.

If you have created a trusting and open environment, this should not be a problem.

2. Don't Abuse Your Power

If people are questioning why certain things are done, or the logic of decisions, never pull rank in response. Your team should feel empowered, if only by you taking the time to explain the rationale for any decisions that have been made.

Your team must be on your side. This will not happen by you telling them that the decision is the right one because you are the boss. Your team may not agree, but they should know why a situation is how it is.

3. Trust Your Team

Your team should be allowed to take actions and make decisions. Trust is a vital component of leadership skills.

If you can't trust people to do their jobs, then you have the wrong people, or you're not managing them properly.

Let them do what they are there to do without peering over their shoulders every fifteen minutes, asking what they are doing with their time.

4. Listen And Act

Truly listening to your team is one of the greatest leadership skills. Good listeners come across as genuinely interested, empathetic, and concerned to find out what's going on. All great leaders have great communication skills.

Unhappy team members can only exist where their problems have not been aired. Create an environment where problems can be discussed so that solutions can be found.

5. Stop Being An Expert On Everything

Leaders often achieve their positions by being proficient in a certain area, and thus will have an opinion on how to fix problems.

They believe it's better to tell someone what to do, or even to do it themselves, than give their team the opportunity to develop their own solutions, and therefore exercise their creativity.

6. Be Constructive

Negativity breeds negativity. How you communicate has a profound effect on your team, as a whole and individually.

Criticisms will always need to be made by leaders, but try to make them constructive, and deliver them without emotional attachment.

7. Judge Your Success By Your Team's

The true success of a leader can be measured by the success of the people who work with and for them.

You cannot be a successful leader of a failing team, just as you cannot be a successful general of a defeated army.

Your focus should always be on building your team's skills and removing obstacles in their way so that they can help you to succeed in achieving the organization goals and objectives.

8. Don't Be A Narcissist

Nothing is more annoying for team members than leaders who make their decisions based on how good it will make them appear to their superiors.

A key leadership skill is integrity. Integrity is about doing the right thing, and allowing praise where praise is due, even if that is not at your door.

9. Have A Sense Of Humour

People work better when they are enjoying themselves. The work itself may be dull, but the environment doe does not have to be. Stifling fun also means stifling creativity.

Team members love it when the leader joins in and has fun. This does not have to create a flippant atmosphere; on the contrary, this is a tenet of team building.

10. Don't Be Too Distant

Without revealing your innermost secrets, it is possible for leaders to show a more human side. If mutual respect exists, this should not be seen as vulnerability, rather a sign that you are a sentient human being, just as your team members are.

Only when your team gets to know the real you will the true foundations of good leadership be properly established – trust and respect.

WRAPPING UP ON LEADERSHIP

Sun Tzu, writing in the 5th century BC in The Art of War said: "What enables the wise sovereign and the good general to strike and conquer and achieve things beyond the reach of ordinary men is foreknowledge."

This is an as-yet-unmentioned attribute of a great leader – the ability to predict. No matter how many managerial and people skills the business leader possesses, they will all be jeopardized if he or she cannot anticipate the effects of the plans they put in place, and the actions they take.

In this respect, it may be that their age and experience must take precedence over consultation with the "troops", who may little understand the ramifications of what is about to take place.

This is where the genuine leader comes to the fore and truly claims their title. When all around are scratching their heads and reluctant to make a decision, old-style leadership must come into play. The modern leader may utterly fail in this scenario for lack of guts and an over-familiarity with their team.

As Sun Tzu says: "Some leaders are generous but cannot use their men. They love their men but cannot command them… These leaders create spoiled children. Their soldiers are useless." Leadership may have become a different beast over the years, but it is still, at its heart, about leading.

With the help of this book, you too can become a great leader. By following the leadership principles within this book. you will be respected for your fairness, your skills and your ability to lead people in a humane but necessary way to achieve greatness with your team.

Leading people can be one of the most rewarding things you've ever done if you do it right. Do it wrong, and leadership can quickly become a nightmare you hope to wake up from sooner than later.

 I hope you enjoyed learning from Leadership - Becoming a Better Leader and look forward to seeing you succeed.

PART TWO: MANAGEMENT

Becoming A Better Manager

CHAPTER 6: MANAGEMENT MASTERY

Welcome to the journey of mastering the art and science of effective management. This part "Becoming a Better Manager" is more than just a part; it's a guide, a companion, and a roadmap toward unlocking your managerial potential.

In today's dynamic and ever-evolving business landscape, the role of a manager is pivotal. It requires a delicate balance of leadership, strategy, empathy, and adaptability. Throughout my career, I've encountered diverse challenges, celebrated successes, weathered storms, and, above all, learned invaluable lessons that have shaped my understanding of what it truly means to be a manager.

This part is born from those experiences—an amalgamation of insights gained from triumphs, setbacks, and the relentless pursuit of improvement. It's a testament to the belief that every challenge presents an opportunity to grow, evolve, and become a better version of ourselves.

Within these pages, you'll embark on a transformative journey. We'll delve into the core principles of effective management, exploring the intricacies of leadership, communication, team dynamics, and the art of balancing tasks and people.

But this isn't just theory; it's a practical guide enriched with real-world approaches, actionable strategies, and tools that you can implement immediately in your managerial role.

From navigating conflicts and inspiring teams to mastering the art of delegation and fostering a culture of innovation, this part aims to equip you with the tools and mindset needed to thrive in the realm of management.

Whether you're a seasoned manager seeking fresh perspectives or someone stepping into their first managerial role, this part is designed to meet you where you are and propel you toward managerial excellence. Each chapter is an invitation to reflect, learn, and adapt—an opportunity to refine your skills and mindset, not just for professional growth but for personal enrichment.

So, join me in this exploration of management mastery, let's embark on a journey that transcends mere management—it's about becoming the kind of leader who inspires, empowers, and brings out the best in teams and individuals.

EXPLORATION OF MANAGEMENT

Many people tend to think of management in terms of the organization of a company, while some regard management as equivalent to business administration and therefore exclude management in places outside the commercial sector.

Management structures are evident throughout society, from government bodies through military forces, and right down to personal home environments.

Management can be defined as all the activities carried out by one or more people with the aim of planning and controlling the activities of other people so that an objective can be achieved that would not have been possible through individuals acting independently.

Management involves organizing, planning, coordinating, and controlling resources within an organization to achieve specific objectives and goals efficiently.

At its core, management is about:

1. Organization And Coordination

Managers organize resources such as people, finances, and materials to ensure tasks are carried out effectively and efficiently.

2. Planning And Decision-Making

Managers engage in strategic planning, setting goals, and outlining the steps needed to achieve those objectives. They make decisions that align with organizational goals and allocate resources accordingly.

3. Implementation And Execution

Managers oversee the execution of plans, ensuring that activities are carried out according to established processes and timelines. They delegate tasks, manage workflows, and monitor progress.

4. Problem-Solving And Decision-Making

Managers tackle challenges and make decisions to address issues that arise within the organization. They use their expertise and judgment to find solutions and navigate obstacles.

5. Leadership And Team Management

While leadership and management are distinct, managers often lead teams and are responsible for guiding and motivating employees to achieve organizational goals.

6. Control and Evaluation

Managers monitor performance, assess outcomes, and ensure that objectives are being met. They may implement control mechanisms to maintain quality standards and efficiency.

Management occurs at various levels within an organization, from frontline supervisors overseeing day-to-day operations to top-level executives setting strategic direction.

It involves a set of skills that encompass planning, organizing, directing, and controlling resources to achieve predetermined objectives and optimize organizational performance.

While leadership and management are often discussed as separate concepts, they are complementary and interdependent.

Effective organizations require strong leadership to set direction and inspire action and efficient management to organize resources and implement plans to achieve that direction.

Many authorities in management believe that there are several parts to the concept of management:

Planning

Organizing

Staffing

Directing

Leading

Controlling

This means that anyone in a managerial role will carry out the above functions of planning, organizing, staffing, directing, leading and controlling to varying degrees, depending on the specific needs, practices, and methods of the organization, and according to the level at which the managing is taking place.

For example, lower-level managers may not have too much input on staffing, as this might be handled by an authority above them. However, a seam that does run through all levels of management is that managers are engaged in getting things done through other people.

This concept, in which all managers perform the same functions of planning, organizing, staffing, directing, leading and controlling at each of their levels, is sometimes called the universality of management.

It is the practices, methods, activities, and tasks within each of these functions that will alter according to the type and purpose of the organization or enterprise.

In the commercial sector, the primary function of management is to satisfy the stakeholders of the company or enterprise. This usually involves making a profit, creating quality products at a reasonable cost, and providing good employment opportunities.

In most management models, shareholders vote for the board of directors, the board then hires the senior management team, which then has the responsibility of putting in place lower levels of management.

FUNCTIONS OF MANAGEMENT

Planning

Planning involves the selection of the organization's goals and ambitions, and formulating the specific actions that will be necessary to achieve them.

This involves a significant degree of decision-making, so that the correct choices can be made once all possibilities have been identified and assessed.

Planning takes in the whole gamut, from the most obvious decisions such as the location of business premises, and employing the right people for the available jobs, right down to the exact details of each component of any manufactured product.

Plans do not become plans until such decisions have been made. Prior to these decisions, managers are analysing, studying, and making proposals.

Organizing

The management function of organizing has at its heart the concept of "role". That is, which employees are to be tasked with carrying out what jobs, and how they are to be put to work.

People working together in teams must know their exact purpose if the organization's objectives are to be realized most efficiently and in the shortest period.

That involves all employees understanding where they fit into the overall picture, and how their job objective contributes to the overall aims.

Management of this function further requires that everyone involved has the appropriate equipment, authority, and information to accomplish the task.

In short, organizing establishes a structure to help create an environment in which human performance can excel. The structure must define the tasks necessary, and the roles must be geared to the abilities of the workers.

Directing

Directing is a fundamental function of management that involves guiding, leading, supervising, and motivating employees to achieve organizational goals.

It's the process of instructing, guiding, and overseeing the work of individuals or teams to ensure that tasks are performed effectively and efficiently.

This function primarily focuses on human aspects within an organization and involves several key elements like communication, motivation, delegation, supervision, goal setting, performance management and conflict resolution.

Managers must convey instructions, expectations, goals, and feedback to their teams. It's crucial to ensure that everyone understands their roles and responsibilities.

Managers must delegate tasks appropriately. Delegation involves assigning responsibilities to individuals based on their skills and strengths, empowering them to take ownership of their work.

Directing includes supervising employees to ensure that they are working according to established standards and procedures. This involves monitoring progress, helping when needed, and ensuring that tasks are completed on time.

Directing includes evaluating employee performance and providing constructive feedback. This helps in identifying strengths and areas for improvement, ultimately contributing to individual and organizational growth.

Addressing conflicts and issues among team members falls under directing. Managers need to facilitate conflict resolution and maintain a harmonious work environment.

Leading

Leading is the managerial function that deals with influencing employees. This requires that the manager possesses interpersonal skills so that their team feels motivated and inspired. Without this influential leadership, employees may feel out of touch with the importance of fulfilling the organization's goals.

Management problems mostly arise from issues with employees. These may be employee conflicts with the manager, employees failing to work together, or individuals suffering behavioural or attitudinal problems.

Managers need to inspire, motivate, and influence their teams to perform at their best. This involves setting a positive example, providing guidance, and fostering a supportive work environment.

Managers must motivate their teams to achieve organizational goals. This may involve recognizing and rewarding good performance, providing opportunities for growth, and creating a motivating work culture. Managers play a pivotal role in setting clear and achievable goals for their teams.

They need to ensure that these goals align with the broader objectives of the organization.

Wherever the problem derives from, it is the manager's job to lead the way out of the mire for all concerned, which means leading from the front. This will require skills in communication, listening, problem-solving, conflict-resolution, and a chameleon-like quality of adapting to the various personalities that populate the workplace.

Controlling

The first part of controlling is monitoring. Effective management involves paying attention to the organization's ongoing plans, and how closely they are being adhered to and their objectives fulfilled.

This will necessitate measuring and perhaps correcting the activities of employees. Without peak human performance, even the best-laid plans are prone to failure. Plans are only the starting point. It is humans who enact them, and humans can become easily distracted or lose motivation.

Although controlling sounds like quite a manipulative process, it is not always the case. It may take as little as a few words of praise or encouragement to keep an employee on track, or it may take formal sanctions and threats of job termination.

Good management means being able to gauge the exact level of control that needs to be exerted to realign performance with objectives.

As effective controlling means monitoring achievement against objectives, the previous issue of organizing becomes important in terms of job roles. Managers need to know exactly who to look at if a certain area is falling behind schedule or missing the mark in any way.

Clearly defined job roles should enable quick identification of the problem source. This not only means it can be easily rectified, but it also avoids the problem of targeting the wrong people as culprits. Criticisms mistakenly levelled at people who are performing well can instantly create new problems in previously model employees.

CHAPTER 7: TRUST AND CONFIDENCE

Trust and confidence are very important in a professional environment for better results. Lack of trust and confidence can lead to a lack of commitment to the cause, which can lead to underperformance and failed objectives.

There are two issues to deal with concerning trust and confidence:

1. Trust In The Organization

Trust in the higher objectives of the organization is crucial; that these objectives are honourable for one, and that they have been planned with foresight and competence. This harks back to the importance of sound planning right at the outset.

The worst outcome of poor managerial planning is that the survival of the organization itself can be jeopardized, which could have clear and dire consequences for all employees.

The moment such doubt exists in an organization, the situation can quickly deteriorate; the saying about "rats leaving a sinking ship" comes to mind.

Trust in the organization at large means building trust in team leadership and vision. Managers and leaders need to be seen to be committed. This allows employees to more readily accept difficult times when they arrive because they feel the correct decisions have been made and the right people are at the helm to weather the storm.

Creating trust and confidence in the organization's objectives necessitates covering all the bases. This means that any new venture must be assessed not just for its merits, but crucially also for its possible pitfalls. Only if these are known can people be confident that the management team has planned for every eventuality.

If there are unknowns in the equation, copious research should be carried out to find as much information as possible, and the worst-case scenario that could result.

Ultimately, there are no foregone conclusions in business, and, by its very nature, trust is not based on cast-iron assurances, rather on the probability that everything will progress in the most pleasing manner.

It is at this point that management must commit itself, reveal its intentions, and ask for the trust of the employees.

2. Trust Amongst Individuals

This is the second area where trust and confidence must be built. In this respect, we are dealing with the day-to-day interactions of the management with its team members, and amongst team members. This is a crucial issue.

Managers must be trusted for their management functions to be realized most effectively, and for their team to gel and become a commercial force to be reckoned with.

The issue of trust in others is an easy one to define. Trusting someone we work with is about having faith in them; believing that they are as good as their word. For managers, it is a matter of having faith in an employee to carry out a task without undue monitoring – knowing that they will not only complete the task when asked, but that they will complete it in line with the stated objectives.

It is also a matter of believing that people will behave acceptably in more general terms. A worker who is excellent at their job but who constantly undermines other members of the team must still be defined as untrustworthy. To be trusted, employees at any level should abide by both company codes of practice and the moral and legal mores that society commonly expects.

Trust makes the working environment easier for everyone and creates the correct atmosphere for the best work to take place. However, if trust is so easily defined and so important, why is it that many managers report that they do not believe they enjoy the trust of the people working under them?

The problem seems to be that trust can be based on outcomes, and when situations are not running smoothly, managers can lose the trust they have created. This suggests that trust was not evident in the first place, because trust is something that should bridge the difficult times.

Trust that disappears when times are hard is extremely fickle and may suggest a larger problem within the organization where overall objectives are not perceived as credible, achievable, or worthwhile. In this case, managers are targeted because they are perceived as being the figurehead of the organization who is easiest to blame, simply because they are most visible.

Talking through issues of trust with employees is a vital part of managerial skills. The effective manager must show they are fully aware that trust is important, and they must seek to identify exactly how trust between themselves and their team, and within their team, can be quantified. This is the only way any problems or shortfalls can be identified.

Managers must nurture trust in their team to ease the flow of communication. Communication is the lifeblood of a healthy organization because it allows the swift identification of problems. It also allows for an atmosphere of honesty to underpin that communication.

Communication of itself is not the goal; the fact that people are talking to each other does not say anything about the quality of that communication. It is open and honest communication that is required, and trust must be the precursor for this to happen.

Employees who trust their managers are more likely to tell them what they need to hear, not what they believe they want to hear. Receiving false information from team members, or receiving the truth too late, could seriously jeopardize the goals of the organization.

A trusting atmosphere also makes for a happy atmosphere. Tensions are reduced when people feel they can trust each other. The overall objectives of a team are achieved by the individual successes of each member, and success is therefore a cumulative and collaborative affair.

One person who cannot be trusted to perform at their best can produce a poisoned workplace because those team members who are fully contributing will feel their efforts are being hampered. The less trusting a team of employees is, the harder their manager will have to work. This alone should be reason enough for any manager to strive to create trust and confidence: for an easier working life.

IDENTIFYING TRUST

Instant trust is certainly possible, but it would be a very gullible individual who adopted such an attitude towards a stranger.
The opposite end of the spectrum is a relationship where both parties have known each other for decades. This is far more common in personal relationships than professional, but such longstanding professional relationships certainly do exist.

However, even in this latter scenario, it is not uncommon for one or both parties to spring some unpleasant surprises after so many years. The longer you know someone, the easier it is to trust them, provided they offer no reasons to make you feel otherwise. When trust is violated in some way, it can disappear forever.

In a professional environment, managers cannot wait decades to establish trust, thus there needs to be monitoring, such as spot checks and behavioural analysis. Although this may give the impression that employees are not to be trusted, there is no other way to effectively monitor for correct behaviour.

The types of behaviour a manager might seek to assess are:

> **Does the employee distort the truth?**

> **Does the employee possess the requisite skills for the job?**

> **Can the employee be left to get on with their job?**

> **Is the employee reliable?**

> **Is the employee prone to gossip and spread rumours?**

> **Will the employee speak up if there is a problem?**

> **Will the employee support fellow colleagues?**

DISTRUST: HOW MANAGERS CREATE IT

As a manager, you need to be aware that you may be responsible for creating distrust in the workplace. These are the most obvious ways in which managers can create distrust between themselves and their team:

- **Inconsistency in communication; saying one thing and doing the opposite.**

- **Inconsistency in how they treat different team members.**

- **Failure to offer clear or honest feedback.**

- **Failure to pass on information pertinent to the team.**

- **Hidden agendas and ulterior motives.**

- **Reluctant to trust other people.**

As a manager, you should lead by example. Negative traits in a manager make it easier for similar traits to appear in their team. An atmosphere of distrust has a hugely negative effect on any workplace, and every effort must be made to employ the tactics that nurture trust.

CHAPTER 8: MANAGER'S PITFALLS

Managing other people has ample rewards when you can see how your team is growing and progressing under your expert governance, but it is easy to get it wrong if you do not pay attention to the following managerial pitfalls:

Failure To Lead By Example

As a manager, you are also a leader, and your team looks to you for guidance. Therefore, you must be careful how you behave in the workplace. You cannot expect other people to behave impeccably when you are not leading by example.

Areas to watch out for are listening respectfully; communicating clearly; accepting ideas from other people; answering questions honestly and willingly.

Delegating Clumsily

Try not to give employees the impression that you are pushing unpalatable work their way by failing to explain exactly why you have chosen a particular individual. Team members have specific roles and like to know that their tasks are theirs because they are best suited to achieving the best outcome.

You must allow them to ask questions so they can understand exactly what their goals are. You should also seek their response to the task, which conveys the message that they have the necessary skill set and you value their input.

They may have ideas that can seriously improve their performance of the task at hand. This is all about motivation. If you can link the task to a specific skill they have, and explain this to them, they will be far more amenable. Everyone loves praise.

Ignoring The Young Blood

This is not only negative for the younger members of the office, but it could also be detrimental to the success of your objectives.

You never know where the next big idea may come from, and it may just be lurking in the freshest minds, precisely because they have not had a chance to be weighed down by the pressure (and possibly tedium) of work.

Don't let personal pride or an ageist attitude blind you to young talent. Spend some time getting to know where the young blood is coming from – how they perceive their strengths and whether they have any great ideas they'd like to share, or tasks they would like to tackle.

Ignoring Older Workers

By the same token, do not ignore your more seasoned workers. They are the ones who have the most experience. They may also have some fresh ideas to offer but may not have the youthful buzz to speak up unless asked.

Make sure you appreciate their skills, which will have been earned over many years.
The fact that you can pretty much leave them alone to get on with things does not mean you should ignore their efforts. Be grateful that they are not a burden to you and are producing the goods.

Older workers who feel taken for granted may "come off the boil" to a certain extent, and thus you risk losing some of your greatest assets in the workplace. As much as their skills may appear set, try to enliven things by offering alternative tasks that may prompt a renewed enthusiasm.

Ordering People About

It may be within your remit to do this, but this should be reserved for those times when employees leave you no choice but to issue orders, if not ultimatums. Try making suggestions and requests rather than issuing orders. It's all semantics, really.

Your team knows that your requests are orders phrased politely, but such subtleties can make a big difference. Remember that your team knows full-well that you have your directives from your own superiors, so will hardly refuse your requests.

If there is a certain latitude in the tasks you are handing out, seek suggestions and encourage employees to share their own ideas on how to best approach matters.

Stifling Creativity

Managers cannot let their workplace, or their team stagnate. To keep the situation fresh, you should be asking for ideas from your team at regular intervals. This not only spawns' new approaches but also shows them that you value their input.

This does not mean abandoning tried and trusted routines that have served the organization for many years; it just means seeing if there are any ways to add a little spice, either with a few new tasks, or with new approaches to old tasks. Businesses thrive on new ideas, and they may even prove to be the impetus to take a business to a whole new level.

Maintaining The Status Quo

The need for fresh ideas is important for managers whose new job is to head an established team. The temptation may be to avoid rocking the boat and to keep a low profile, but dynamic leadership may be part of the reason you have been called in.

Although you will not want to change routines that the organization depends upon, you should not be afraid to try a few new working practices to see how they pan out and how they may benefit your team's productivity.

Storing Up Problems

This relates specifically to the practice of noting personnel problems in a log to be delivered en masse during staff supervision or appraisals. This can be detrimental for several reasons.

Problems that are allowed to carry on may damage productivity; the team members at fault will resent the fact that they were allowed to continue in error for so long; they may be confronted with a long list of problems that could damage their confidence; and your ability to create trust will have been tarnished, because you failed to communicate the truth when it was necessary.

It is far better to deal with issues as they arise to minimize damage and show the team that you are a sharp manager who will not any situation drift. Staff appraisals are not designed as a delivery system for months of problems; rather they are used to monitor staff behaviour and performance over that time, which should include the ability to take on board advice and direction as and when.

Taking Highfliers For Granted

This is a similar problem to ignoring the young blood and workplace veterans. The danger here is more pronounced, however, because a failure to properly praise and reward your stars may lead to them seeking better and more remunerative employment elsewhere, and these high achievers may be contributing a disproportionate amount of success to your overall figures.

Losing them would therefore be a serious blow not just to your team, but to the entire organization. You do not want to be the one who is blamed for losing your team's biggest asset. Make sure these people know you value them, and if that means increasing their income, then that will be a small price to pay for keeping them on your side.

Focusing on the negative rather than the positive. Everyone makes mistakes, but concentrating solely on mistakes whilst ignoring the positives is guaranteed to alienate employees. Although you may believe that a job well done is only to be expected, yes, it is always a good idea to praise team members who perform well.

That is the way to encourage more behaviour of the same sort. It doesn't take much effort to congratulate someone, but it can have a huge impact on their attitude. A team member who consistently excels and is not praised may end up losing interest. Where praise is neglected and criticisms levelled, this can be the cause of serious resentment.

This does not mean that you cannot point out mistakes, but it is better to surround the criticism with points that you do admire about that person's work. This serves to cushion the negative comment, and subtly suggests that they should exchange their mistake for further success.

Failing To Build A Strong Team

Managers should remember to nurture a team ethos. Individuals within a team work better together when they are more aware of belonging to a team. A sense of team creates a more powerful force than the idea that a workplace is just a gathering of individuals.

This can be encouraged by holding regular team meetings where everyone has a chance to express their views and share exactly what they are doing to contribute to the whole team effort.

CHALLENGES IN MANAGING PEOPLE

Managing people can be immensely rewarding, but it also comes with its fair share of challenges. Below are some of the common challenges that managers face when managing and leading teams:

Team Dynamics

Building cohesive and high-performing teams involves understanding individual strengths, weaknesses, and personalities. Balancing team dynamics, addressing cliques, and fostering collaboration can be challenging.

Adapting To Change

Managing people through organizational changes, such as restructuring, new policies, or technological advancements, requires effective change management skills. Resistance to change can impact productivity and morale.

Employee Engagement And Motivation

Keeping employees engaged, motivated, and satisfied requires ongoing effort. Addressing disengagement, low morale, or burnout can be challenging.

Communication Breakdowns

Ensuring effective communication across diverse teams with varying communication styles, preferences, and understanding levels can be challenging. Misunderstandings, unclear instructions, and lack of transparent communication can hinder productivity.

Conflict Resolution

Managing conflicts that arise among team members or departments requires tact and skill. Resolving disagreements and maintaining a harmonious work environment can be demanding.

Diversity And Inclusion

Managing diverse teams and fostering an inclusive workplace requires awareness, sensitivity, and efforts to ensure everyone feels valued and respected.

Retention And Talent Development

Retaining top talent and developing employees' skills to meet evolving needs are ongoing challenges. Ensuring growth opportunities and a conducive work environment is essential for talent retention.

Performance Management

Evaluating and managing the performance of team members while providing constructive feedback can be complex. Balancing the need for accountability and maintaining team morale can be a delicate task.

Developing Leadership Skills

As a manager, continually developing leadership skills and adapting to new management techniques and best practices is crucial. The need to evolve and stay updated in a rapidly changing work landscape can be demanding.

Workload Management

Ensuring that workloads are distributed fairly among team members while maintaining efficiency and avoiding burnout is a constant challenge.

Remote Work Challenges

Managing remote or hybrid teams adds another layer of complexity. Overcoming communication barriers, maintaining team cohesion, and ensuring productivity can be more challenging in remote settings.

Summary Of Challenges In Managing People

Addressing these challenges requires a combination of strong interpersonal skills, adaptability, effective communication, empathy, and strategic thinking.

Managers who can navigate these challenges often contribute significantly to the success and well-being of their teams and organizations.

CHAPTER 9: TEAM SPIRIT

Without a team spirit, organizations can suffer. No matter how well-organized and planned a venture may be, without the commitment of the team behind it, the objectives will not be as effectively or as quickly met.

Building team spirit is about engaging the emotions of the team members. It is more than a cerebral idea that a team is more than the sum of its parts; it is truly feeling that you are a part of something worthwhile, and that everyone is working together to make a success of things.

There should be a sense of enjoyment at being amongst your colleagues, and so much the better if that happy relationship extends beyond the workplace to recreational activities. Having a team spirit means that problems do not escalate due to the impact of conflicting personalities.

Even if there are personality clashes, a team spirit will serve to reduce their negative effects because the individuals concerned should have as their overriding concern the wellbeing and emotional health of the team. Differences can be put to one side for the greater good.

HOW TO BUILD TEAM SPIRIT

Below are some of the areas a manager should look at when considering how to build team spirit:

1. Cooperation

Cooperation amongst team members should be encouraged, and forming smaller groups that work together on tasks and projects can help to promote closer working relationships.

In this way, team members are directly involved with each other's work, and fully aware of how all the parts contribute to the whole.

2. Clear The Decks

Clear the decks of unnecessary clutter by identifying all the extra bureaucracy and paperwork and tasks that detract from the job at hand and thus reduce motivation.

A team spirit cannot be engendered in individuals whose focus is on petty matters. This may not be easy in this age of double and triple checking, but if such matters are unavoidable, try and find ways for employees outside the team to cover them, or attend to them yourself.

3. Build Strong Relationship

Building strong relationships between the organization and its customers and encourage customer feedback so that your team can appreciate the positive effects they are having.

Try to involve customers in company events for face to-face feedback opportunities. Make sure that upper management does not remain aloof, but make sure they are also involved in passing on positive feedback wherever possible.

4. Allow Your Team Some Autonomy

As much as you are the manager of the team, your team may not regard you as being a part of their operation. Just as in sports, there is a separation between the team and their manager; the team is primed by the manager and then allowed to work their magic.

This is a useful lesson for the business world. This should clearly not reach the point where your word lacks authority, but your team should certainly be allowed to carry on with minimal interference if they are on target for their given objectives.

In the same way, do not impose too many rules and regulations just for the sake of having them in place to prove your authority. The confident manager can easily step back and know their influence remains intact.

5. Make The Workplace Enjoyable

Managers should not be reluctant to inject humour into the situation for fear of creating a flippant atmosphere.
Trust that your team is mature enough to know when enough is enough.

A sure-fire way to damage team spirits is by trying to enforce a dour mood, thinking that this is the only way to keep your team focused on important matters. This is insulting to your team. It is quite possible to have a sense of humour and a serious attitude towards work.

In fact, the former positively encourages the latter, as it provides an essential counterbalance. It is unreasonable to expect that your team should be deadpan the whole day. Humour helps to release the tensions that can build from hard work, and it can help free a little creativity into the bargain. Just make sure that the humour is healthy, and does not, in certain cases, shift into personal put-downs.

6. Be Open About Yourself

This does not mean wheeling in a couch and recounting your whole life story, but your team will be encouraged to know that you understand their feelings because you were perhaps once in their shoes, and they will also appreciate the trust you have placed in them by not keeping a professional distance.

Showing your human side can encourage your team members to lower their own barriers, and the more affinity they feel for each other on a human level, the better they will work with each other.

7. Strive To Avoid Disagreements

This can be dealt with by maintaining and encouraging communication. There will always be times when even the best of teams suffers a little internal misunderstanding, but this should not be a problem if all parties are able to freely talk about how they perceive the problem arose and offer suggestions on how it may be resolved.

Managers must be realistic in this respect, and not think that there should be perfect peace and harmony within their team. If this appears to be the case, team members may feel reluctant to speak out and any grievances will continue to simmer.

8. Recognize And Celebrate

It is good to recognize and celebrate when objectives are achieved. Team spirits can be lifted when their work results in the attainment of their objectives. Managers should not let these moments pass unannounced. It may be possible to organize from the budget some team rewards that mark such achievements. Nevertheless, even daily triumphs should be congratulated. Remember that a little praise goes a long way.

PROBLEM EMPLOYEES: HOW TO TACKLE IT

The problems caused by one employee can easily undermine the achievements and positive attitude of the team. Although the ultimate sanction is terminating the individual's employment, there are steps to take before reaching that stage.

1. Hire The Right People

Problem employees should not be a big issue if sufficient resources and time have been spent in the candidate selection process. This means that references should always be taken up with previous employers, and the candidate's job history scrutinized.

Frequent changes in employment can indicate either a restless individual who does not easily settle, or someone who is "encouraged" to move on from jobs. Problem employees are not always fired; in fact, the conditions for getting rid of a troublesome soul may include giving them an unreasonably creditable reference.

2. Confront The Problem

Managers must deal with problems as they arise, and not wait for the official evaluation process to address issues. It may be that the individual does not realize the problems they are causing, and it only takes a moment to point it out and effectively remedy the situation. However, before this moment happens, the manager should prepare on how to confront the problem.

3. Investigate The Problem

Although some problems will be glaringly obvious, others may not even be apparent to the manager until another team member speaks up. Bear in mind that the word of one person should not damn another's reputation.

If only one person perceives there to be a problem, you may be dealing with a personality clash where both parties are to blame. It is essential that you do your homework to establish the facts.

Gossip and hearsay are not a good basis for taking disciplinary action, even on the most informal level. Make sure you have exhausted all sources of information before you confront an employee. Managers need to be sure of their ground.

5. Plan Your Approach

The smart manager will ensure that they have planned how they will deal with the problem employee. This involves making enough time, choosing the right time, selecting a place where you won't be interrupted, and considering whether you need an HR representative present.

You should also avoid calling employees out of the workplace in full sight of the rest of the team. This is embarrassing and is a terrible start to any discussion.

6. Assess If You Are Part Of The Problem

It may be that the problem has been partly caused by the manager who is about to confront the situation. This will only exacerbate the problem. Few employees will feel able to openly criticize their manager for fear of reprisals, but unless such resentments are brought out into the open, the situation cannot improve.

Managers must be humble enough to realize when they are contributing to the problem and must request that the employee is perfectly honest about how they feel. Managers need to ask themselves: do they want to be right, or do they want peace?

7. Use The Evaluation Process

As mentioned, you should not wait for this official overview of performance to act, but this does provide a useful hiatus in which you can assess the direction in which an employee is heading. It is here that expectations can be officially set for the following period, which means the employee is left in no doubt regarding what is now required of them.

8. Do Not Tolerate Negativity

It may be that an employee is producing good work because this reflects in their pay, but such person is a negative influence on the rest of the team due to their general attitude.

Great results do not mitigate a lousy attitude. Attitudes can be infectious, and any negativity should be stamped on the moment it appears lest it spreads throughout the workplace.

9. See The Bigger Picture

You must try to recognize when problems are being caused wilfully or accidentally. Everyone experiences unhappy times in their lives that are down to situations outside the workplace.

Managers must be sensitive to the possibility that the problem employee may be during some personal crisis and is not just behaving badly for the hell of it. As you talk with the employee, listen carefully to what they have to say, don't be judgmental, and don't interrupt.

If you can find out what the real source of the problem behaviour is, you have a much better chance of finding a solution.

11. Deal With The Behaviour, Not The Person

This follows on from the previous point, in that a negative attitude does not equate to a negative person. Behaviours and attitudes are often short-lived and almost always correctable. Never damn the individual by attacking them personally. Understand that the behaviour is not the person.

12. Pay Attention To Your Language

The way in which a manager addresses a problem individual can dictate how the situation plays out. The initial approach should be diplomatically made with positive language and expression. An attacking demeanour will generally lead to an escalation of negative feelings in the employee.

13. Find A Solution

The result of your discussion should be to find a way forward to resolve the problem. This should not always be imposed by the manager; rather the employee should be asked to suggest ways in which the situation can improve, thus being given the chance to "own" the solution.

14. Monitor The Situation

Remain attentive to the situation and make sure the problem is getting better, and that it has not simply dipped beneath the radar for a while.

15. Last Resort

Where official disciplinary action or dismissal is called for, make certain that everything is done by the book and records of the issues and how you have tried to help duly kept. Be mindful of relevant statutes and seek legal advice if necessary.

CHAPTER 10: EMOTIONAL INTELLIGENCE

Emotional intelligence is the ability to perceive, control, and evaluate emotions – your own and those of other people. This is a relatively new area of study that is giving long overdue importance to the idea that the emotional part of our brains can have a significant impact on how successfully we live our lives and how well we interact with other people.

Any manager worth his salt should therefore be an expert on emotional intelligence. If you are not able to keep a reign on your own emotions, and find that they are pulling you way daily, how can you possibly expect to exert the slightest positive influence on other people?

Emotional Intelligence Areas To Focus On

1. Emotional Awareness

This is the ability to correctly identify our core emotions when they appear. These will include anger, sadness, fear, joy, frustration, etc. It is also crucial that you can spot these in other people, especially as there may be attempts to disguise them.

2. Emotional Self-Management

This is the ability to control our emotions and express them in an appropriate manner. This is something that every effective manager should be able to master if they hope to maintain a professional workplace demeanour.

Having a temper tantrum in the middle of the office because targets have been missed will destroy your credibility as a leader and cause a certain amount of amusement.

3. Emotional Flexibility

This is the ability to recover from stress, loss, and shocking events that have damaged your emotional equilibrium. This is crucial if you are to be viewed as an effective leader.

Sitting in your office weeping for days when something goes wrong is hardly likely to inspire confidence in your team. This is about learning from the past, but not carrying it around with you so it colours how you live life in the present.

DECISION MAKING

Managers make decisions daily. Using emotional intelligence in making decisions involves striking a balance between your thinking brain and your emotional brain.

Mostly in business, your thinking brain will inform your decisions because they will need to be made based on pure facts. However, there may be times when there are two equally balanced options, and it is then that your emotional intelligence may sway the decision on the power of your gut reaction.

Leading people using emotional intelligence is all about leading by example. Your team will be looking to you for guidance and inspiration.

We are all subject to the emotional rollercoaster, that is life, and there may be nothing we can do to forestall unpleasant events from occurring that disrupt our equilibrium. But where we cannot determine certain outcomes, we can certainly try to control how we react to them.

Emotional intelligence is not about stifling your emotions and becoming an automaton, but rather about using your emotions to create more positive outcomes. Emotions are vital in business because they are the passions that motivate us to achieve more.

Positive emotions provide the furnace that powers the business you are involved in. If you can control your emotions and channel positivity into your managerial role, it will be a struggle for any of your team to respond in the opposite way.

Lee Iacocca, former CEO of Chrysler, said: *"Management is nothing more than motivating other people."*

Although management is clearly far more than motivation, this encapsulates the emotional essence of the skill. We can talk all we like about the management functions of planning, organizing, directing, leading and controlling, but these say little about the human aspect of managing, which is dealing with people on a day-to-day basis.

Motivation is crucial in the workplace because our working lives take up such a massive chunk of our lives in general, and truth be told, most of us would give up our regular jobs if we won the jackpot.

In some ways, however, Iacocca's statement is rather glib, as it simplistically deals with the perfect scenario. Creating the right conditions for motivation to be possible is far more challenging. Effective management involves building a powerful skill set that cannot be learned by rote from a book.

Management is about dealing with people in the most effective manner. Such abilities may come more naturally to some than others, but the dynamics of the average workplace require that managers are able to instinctively respond correctly, whatever the situation.

CHAPTER 11: TRANSFORM TO A LEADER

Transforming Managers Into Inspirational Leaders

If you are ready to take your team to new heights and inspire greatness? The journey from being a manager to becoming a true leader begins here.

Managers oversee tasks and processes, but leaders inspire, motivate, and guide their teams to success. In today's ever-evolving business landscape, leadership is the key to driving innovation, fostering a positive work culture, and achieving exceptional results.

Your transformation from a manager to leader have started. Now, embark fully on a journey of self-discovery, growth, and empowerment.

This book is comprehensive and has all it takes to empower managers to unleash their leadership potential. There are proven strategies, real-world insights, and actionable techniques to help you:

➢ **Develop a Vision: Learn to create a compelling vision that energizes and unites your team.**

➢ **Inspire Others: Discover how to lead by example and inspire your team to perform at their best.**

> **Communicate Effectively: Hone your communication skills to connect with your team on a deeper level.**

> **Cultivate Resilience: Develop the mental strength to lead through challenges and uncertainty. Foster Innovation: Encourage creativity and innovation within your team.**

Implementing the leadership styes and approaches discussed in this book we shape you into the inspirational leader your team deserves.

Absence Of Inspirational Leaders

Here are ten common problems and pains that organizations may face if they do not invest in transforming their managers into inspirational leaders:

Lack Of Vision

Without inspirational leaders, teams may lack a clear and motivating vision, making it difficult to align and work toward common goals.

Low Morale

Teams led by uninspiring managers may suffer from low morale, decreased motivation, and a negative work environment.

Reduced Productivity

A lack of inspiration and motivation can lead to decreased productivity and lower performance levels.

High Turnover

Managers who do not inspire may struggle to retain top talent, leading to high employee turnover and the associated costs.

Ineffective Communication

Poor communication can lead to misunderstandings, misalignment, and decreased productivity.

Missed Innovation

Without inspirational leadership, innovation may suffer, and teams might miss opportunities for growth and improvement.

Resistance To Change

Inspiring leaders can help teams adapt to change more effectively. Without them, resistance to change can be more common.

Stagnation

Teams led by managers who don't inspire may stagnate, resulting in missed opportunities for growth and development.

Conflict And Disengagement

Teams may experience more conflict and disengagement when not led by inspirational leaders who foster collaboration and engagement.

Limited Success

Organizations may not reach their full potential or achieve their strategic objectives without leaders who can inspire and drive success.

Investing in leadership excellence and transforming managers into inspirational leaders can help address these challenges and create a more dynamic, motivated, and successful organization.

Similarities Between Leadership And Management

Leadership and management share several similarities as they are interconnected and often overlap in organizational contexts. Here are some key similarities:

Influence And Direction

Leaders influence and guide individuals or teams toward a shared vision or goal. They inspire and motivate, setting the direction for the organization.

Managers also influence, providing direction through planning, organizing, and coordinating resources to achieve specific objectives and goals.

Goal Achievement

Leaders are focused on achieving long-term goals, often by inspiring others to embrace a compelling vision and work towards common objectives.

Managers work towards achieving short-term and long-term goals by planning, organizing, and coordinating resources effectively.

Decision-Making

Leaders make strategic decisions that align with the organization's vision and long-term objectives. They often take calculated risks to drive innovation and change.

Managers make operational decisions to ensure tasks are carried out efficiently and in accordance with organizational plans.

People Skills

Leaders require strong interpersonal and communication skills to build relationships, inspire trust, and foster a positive organizational culture.

Managers also need people skills to lead teams effectively, provide support, and ensure that tasks are executed with the collaboration of team members.

Adaptability

Leaders are often at the forefront of driving change and adaptation. They encourage innovation and are open to new ideas and approaches.
Managers must be adaptable to changing circumstances and able to implement changes effectively within their teams or departments.

Accountability

Leaders are accountable for the overall direction and success of the organization. They are responsible for the vision and the impact on the organizational culture.

Managers are accountable for the effective use of resources, meeting goals, and ensuring that tasks are carried out as planned.

While leadership and management have these similarities, it's crucial to recognize their unique aspects and the specific roles they play in an organization.

Both are essential for the overall success and effectiveness of an organization, and the best outcomes often result from a balanced integration of strong leadership and effective management.

Differences Between Leadership And Management

The distinction between leadership and management lies in their focus, approach, and the outcomes they aim to achieve within an organization:

Focus

Leadership is primarily about inspiring and influencing others toward a shared vision or goal. It involves setting a direction, motivating people, and fostering innovation and change.

Management is more about organizing, planning, coordinating, and controlling resources within an organization to achieve specific objectives and goals efficiently.

Approach

Leaders focus on empowering individuals, encouraging personal growth, and inspiring others to achieve beyond what's expected. They often exhibit visionary thinking, empathy, and the ability to rally people around a common purpose.

Managers focus on implementing processes, ensuring tasks are accomplished, and maintaining stability and order within the organization. They often emphasize adherence to procedures, resource allocation, and problem-solving.

Outcome

The outcome of effective leadership is often marked by creating a sense of direction, aligning people with a vision, fostering a positive organizational culture, and promoting long-term growth and development.

The outcome of effective management involves meeting established goals, ensuring operational efficiency, controlling costs, and maintaining stability within the organization.

In summary, leadership emphasizes vision, inspiration, and driving change, while management focuses on organization, efficiency, and implementation. Effective organizations often require a blend of strong leadership and efficient management to thrive.

Leaders set the direction and inspire action, while managers organize resources, implement plans, and ensure operational success within that direction. Both functions are crucial and complementary in achieving overall organizational success.

LEADERSHIP EXCELLENCE

"Exceptional Leader", the journey embarked upon within these pages culminates in a transformative realization: the synergy between managerial prowess and inspirational leadership.

Throughout this book, the focus has been on embracing the qualities, strategies, and mindset necessary to excel in both domains, blending the art of management with the essence of leadership.

This book stands as a guide, offering insights and tools to navigate the complex landscape of modern leadership and management. It empowers readers to evolve, grow, and emerge as catalysts for positive change, not only within their professional spheres but also in their broader communities and the world at large.

Ultimately, "Exceptional Leader" challenges leaders, managers, aspiring individuals and readers to embrace their roles with enthusiasm, commitment, and a dedication to leaving a positive impact.

It serves as a testament to the transformative power of combining managerial prowess with inspirational leadership, paving the way for personal and organizational excellence.

The final chapter encapsulates the essence of this holistic approach, emphasizing the critical components that bridge the gap between management and leadership. The emphasis rests on the integration of managerial acumen with the visionary qualities of leadership. It underlines the significance of:

Integrated Leadership And Management

Recognizing the symbiotic relationship between effective management and inspirational leadership. Understanding that while management ensures operational efficiency and organizational structure, leadership instils purpose, vision, and motivation within teams.

Visionary Management

Infusing managerial practices with visionary thinking. Understanding that effective management isn't solely about processes and structures but also about crafting a vision that resonates with teams, aligning their efforts toward a common goal.

Empowerment And Direction

Empowering individuals not just to perform tasks efficiently but also to contribute ideas, innovate, and grow. Acknowledging the significance of providing clear direction while fostering an environment where individuals feel valued and inspired to excel.

Balanced Decision-Making

Embracing a balanced approach to decision-making that integrates the strategic foresight of leadership with the pragmatic execution of management. Recognizing that decisions should align with the organization's vision while also ensuring practical implementation.

Continuous Growth And Adaptability

Understanding that the journey to becoming a better manager and leader is a continuous process of growth and adaptation. Embracing change, learning from experiences, and constantly evolving to meet the demands of a dynamic environment.

CONCLUSION

The conclusion of this book serves as an invitation—a call to action—for leaders, managers and aspiring individuals to integrate the best of both worlds: the precision and efficacy of managerial expertise and the inspiration and vision of leadership.
It challenges readers not merely to lead or manage but to do both seamlessly, catalysing positive change and fostering growth within themselves and their teams.

As the final page turns, it marks the beginning of a new chapter—one where the distinction between management and leadership fades, giving rise to a holistic approach that unleashes potential, drives innovation, and cultivates an environment where both individuals and organizations thrive. The journey to Becoming Exceptional Leader isn't just a destination—it's an ongoing commitment to excellence, growth, and the pursuit of an impactful legacy, and with dedication, you can become an exceptional leader.

ATTENTION: Thank you for your purchase!

If you are unhappy with your career or with people you are working with or leading, then I'd like to help you create a career breakthrough. I invite you to take advantage of a special, "Free Career Breakthrough" coaching session where we'll work together to…

1. Create a crystal-clear vision for your "ultimate career success" and the "perfect lifestyle" you'd like your career to provide.

2. Uncover hidden challenges that may be sabotaging your career growth and keeping you working too many hours with stress, overwhelm and burnout.

3. You will leave the session renewed, re-energized, and inspired to turn your career around for good with a flourishing personal life.

Call 02035070245, WhatsApp 07432319764 or email ray@connectoptions.co.uk

Connect with me on social media and ask me any question…… www.facebook.com/raykene www.instagram.com/raykene1, www.linkedin.com/in/raykene

RAY KENE
Leadership & Success Mentor

AUTHOR – RAY KENE

Ray Kene, author of Choose and Determine To Succeed, is a leadership and success mentor. For over twenty years, Ray has been in leadership and management in various capacities with different organizations.

He has used his skills and dynamic personality through his words, performance, coaching and mentoring to help, improve and change teams, organizations and individual lives around the world.

Ray is an expert in leadership & management strategies, performance strategies, productive strategies and profitable strategies. He knows how to boost a business's bottom line for sustainable growth and how to guide individuals to success.

Ray is a motivational and inspirational speaker with style, substance and charisma, what he says makes a difference and changes life. He is acknowledged as distinguished and preeminent coach and mentor on leadership, management, wealth, success and happiness.

To Your Success!
Ray Kene
Leadership & Success Mentor

www.connectoptions.co.uk